Contents

KT-119-087

Good manners

People with good manners know
how to behave in different places.

Oh, Behave!

Manners at School

Siân Smith

Bromley Libraries

30128 80112 163 6

www.raintreepublishers.co.uk
Visit our website to find out more information about Raintree books.

To order:
☎ Phone 0845 6044371
🖨 Fax +44 (0) 1865 312263
📧 Email myorders@raintreepublishers.co.uk

Customers from outside the UK please telephone +44 1865 312262

Raintree is an imprint of Capstone Global Library Limited, a company incorporated in England and Wales having its registered office at 7 Pilgrim Street, London, EC4V 6LB – Registered company number: 6695582

Text © Capstone Global Library Limited 2013
First published in hardback in 2013
First published in paperback in 2014
The moral rights of the proprietor have been asserted.

All rights reserved. No part of this publication may be reproduced in any form or by any means (including photocopying or storing it in any medium by electronic means and whether or not transiently or incidentally to some other use of this publication) without the written permission of the copyright owner, except in accordance with the provisions of the Copyright, Designs and Patents Act 1988 or under the terms of a licence issued by the Copyright Licensing Agency, Saffron House, 6–10 Kirby Street, London EC1N 8TS (www.cla.co.uk). Applications for the copyright owner's written permission should be addressed to the publisher.

Edited by Dan Nunn, Rebecca Rissman, and John-Paul Wilkins
Designed by Marcus Bell
Picture research by Elizabeth Alexander
Production by Alison Parsons
Originated by Capstone Global Library Ltd
Printed and bound in China by Leo Paper Products Ltd

ISBN 978 1 406 23821 1 (hardback)
16 15 14 13 12
10 9 8 7 6 5 4 3 2 1

ISBN 978 1 406 23826 6 (paperback)
17 16 15 14 13
10 9 8 7 6 5 4 3 2 1

British Library Cataloguing in Publication Data
Smith, Siân.
Manners at school. -- (Oh, behave!)
395.5-dc22
A full catalogue record for this book is available from the British Library.

Acknowledgements
We would like to thank the following for permission to reproduce photographs: © Capstone Publishers pp. 7, 15, 16, 17, 22 (Karon Dubke); © Corbis p. 8; Alamy p. 19 (© Bubbles Photolibrary); Corbis pp. 9, 23 (© Tomas Rodriguez); Getty Images pp. 4 (Rayes/Digital Vision), 6 (Jonathan Kirn/Riser), 11, 22 (Floresco Productions/Cultura), 13, 22 (Rubberball/Nicole Hill), 21 (Superstudio/The Image Bank); iStockphoto pp. 14, 22 (© Christopher Futcher), 23 (© Julia Savchenko); Shutterstock pp. 5, 23 (© Darrin Henry), 10, 12, 18, 20 (© Monkey Business Images).

Front cover photograph of schoolgirls pulling faces reproduced with permission of Shutterstock (© StockLite). Rear cover photograph of three children reading together reproduced with permission of Shutterstock (© Darrin Henry).

Every effort has been made to contact copyright holders of material reproduced in this book. Any omissions will be rectified in subsequent printings if notice is given to the publisher.

We would like to thank Nancy Harris and Dee Reid for their assistance in the preparation of this book.

If you have good manners, people
will enjoy having you at school.

At school

Hold doors open for other people.

Don't shut the door without looking.

Move quietly around school.

If you are noisy you will disturb people.

In class

Listen to the person who is talking.

Don't talk when you should be listening.

Say "please" and "thank you" when you ask for help.

Don't mess around or upset people.

Wait for your turn.

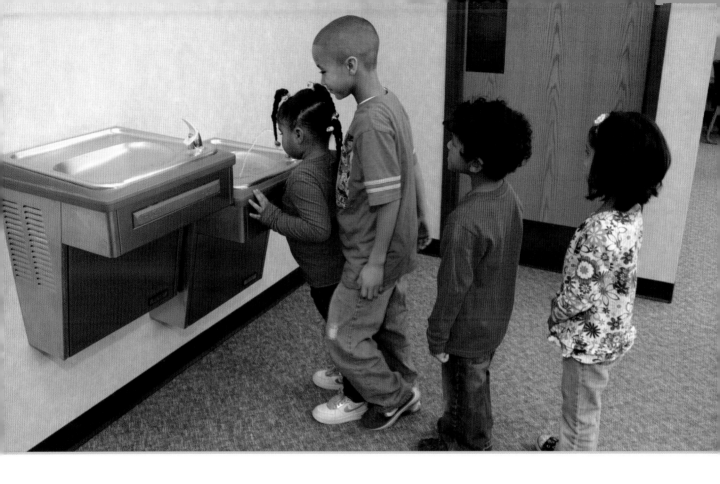

Don't push in front of other people.

Ask if you need to borrow something.

Don't take other people's things.

In the playground

Ask people if they would like to play.

Don't leave people out of
your games.

All the time

Say nice things when you are with other people.

Treat people the way you like to be treated.

Best behaviour

Who here has good manners?

Answer on page 24

Picture glossary

borrow to use something that belongs to someone else

disturb do something that stops people from doing what they need to do

good manners ways of behaving politely and well

Index

Answer to question on page 22
The children with their hands up waiting for the teacher have good manners.

Notes for parents and teachers

Before reading
Explain that good manners are ways of behaving – they help us to understand what to do and how to act. They are important because they show us how to treat each other and help us to get on well with other people. What examples of good manners can the children think of? List these together.

After reading
- What manners do the children think are important in school? Agree a class list of the most important ones together. Phrase each manner in a positive way (for example "ask if you can borrow things" rather than "don't snatch"). Create a book of these good manners. Children can take photographs of the manners being shown in class to illustrate the book.
- Play a manners drawing game. Draw some pictures on the board that show manners at school. Ask the children to guess what is being shown. Role-play could be used instead of drawing if the manners are harder to demonstrate through drawings.